Cambridge English Readers

Level 1

Series editor: Philip Prowse

Three Tomorrows

Frank Brennan

T0134249

CAMBRIDGE
UNIVERSITY PRESS

CAMBRIDGE
UNIVERSITY PRESS

University Printing House, Cambridge CB2 8BS, United Kingdom

One Liberty Plaza, 20th Floor, New York, NY 10006, USA

477 Williamstown Road, Port Melbourne, VIC 3207, Australia

314–321, 3rd Floor, Plot 3, Splendor Forum, Jasola District Centre, New Delhi – 110025, India

79 Anson Road, #06–04/06, Singapore 079906

Cambridge University Press is part of the University of Cambridge.

It furthers the University's mission by disseminating knowledge in the pursuit of education, learning and research at the highest international levels of excellence.

www.cambridge.org
Information on this title: www.cambridge.org/9780521693776

First published 2006

Frank Brennan has asserted his right to be identified as the Author of the Work in accordance with the Copyright, Design and Patents Act 1988.

Printed in Great Britain by Ashford Colour Press Ltd.

Illustrations by Chris Pavely

A catalogue record for this publication is available from the British Library

ISBN 978-0-521-69377-6 Paperback

Contents

Spam

Time: five years from now
Place: England

'Oh no!' said Joe Turner. 'When I go on the computer, all I get is spam – email that nobody wants. It's all from people who are trying to sell you things. Email which is trying to get money from you. Email that says it can help your love life. Email that says it can make you rich. It's just stupid! And do I ask for any of it? No! It's all spam, spam, spam! I can't get emails from my friends and from my work because I've got too much spam. All I get is spam, spam and more spam! It takes a long time to get spam off my computer too. Sometimes I lose important emails because I get so angry!'

'Dad, don't get angry,' said Louise, his daughter. She loved her father. He made her laugh, but he didn't like computers. They made him angry. 'Everybody gets spam, Dad. There's nothing we can do about it. Just live with it,' Louise said.

'It's easy for you, Louise,' Joe answered. 'You're a teenager. Fourteen-year-old girls all use computers these days. You know all about them. But not me. I remember when there was no spam. I can even remember when we didn't have a computer. Oh, happy days!'

'Dad, I live with spam, that's all. Everybody lives with it now. I don't know why you don't. Mum does.'

Joe laughed. 'Ha! You know why? She doesn't use the computer much. That's why. And what does she do when something goes wrong on the computer? She asks one of us to do something about it. Remember last week? She opened some spam and it had a virus! You can't use a computer when there's a virus on it. We worked for hours to make it OK again.'

'What do you mean, *we*?' said Louise. 'You mean me, Dad. You just watched. I did all the work.'

'I was there to help,' replied Joe with big, open eyes. 'I'm always there to help you. You know that.'

'Thanks, Dad,' Louise answered with a smile. 'That's good to know.'

Two weeks later, Joe looked at the news on the internet and ate his breakfast. His wife, Inez, was there with Louise. It was eight o'clock in the morning.

'Yes!' he shouted. 'They did it! This is what we need!'

Inez often heard her husband shout when he read the news. 'What did they do, Joe?' she asked.

'Computer experts can stop spam!' laughed Joe. 'That's what they say in the news. And the good thing is – it isn't going to cost us anything! The computer experts say spam's going to stop. Isn't that great?'

Louise sat up. 'Just a minute, Dad. Do you mean that we aren't going to find spam on the computer again? And we don't need to pay anything? That's really good! But how can they do that?'

'I don't know,' said Joe. 'Is it going to work? That's the important thing!'

Inez looked happy, too. She didn't like computers, but she *hated* spam!

Joe and his family hated spam. But it wasn't only them. There were many people everywhere who hated it too. Millions of them got the free software and used it to stop spam. It worked. People only got the emails that they wanted. Everybody was happy. Spam was gone.

That's what they thought.

*   *   *

Louise went on a camping holiday with her school friends. 'No more computers or television for three weeks! What am I going to do?' she laughed.

When Louise was on holiday, her parents heard some news about a new internet shopping company. This company sold everything. 'Wait for emails from our internet company. Our prices are cheap and there's something for everybody. We're the best internet shopping company in the world!' said the person on the television.

That evening, Joe and Inez read the emails from the internet shopping company. Lots of people from all over England read the emails. Everyone wanted the cheap prices.

Three weeks later
'Now why did you buy that?' asked Joe Turner.

Inez looked at her new salad bowl and put it on the kitchen table. There were four more bowls on the table. They were all the same.

'I don't know,' she said. 'But when I see a salad bowl like this, I want to buy it. I feel bad when I don't. I don't know why. Funny, isn't it?'

'What, more things for the garden, Dad?' laughed Louise. She was at home again, after her holiday. 'Our flat's on the fourth floor, remember? There's no garden here!'

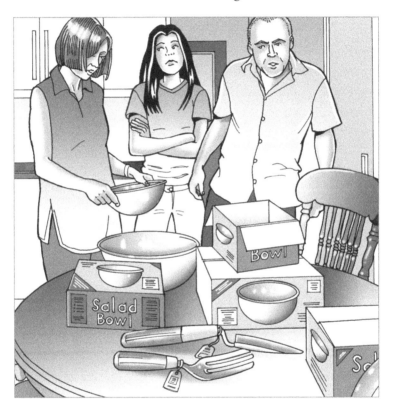

'I just forget when I see them,' said Joe. 'I can't stop. I want to buy them all the time!'

And that wasn't all. Joe and Inez had lots of other things, too. They didn't need any of them. Louise saw that. But it didn't stop her parents. There was shopping everywhere in the flat. Louise knew something was wrong. But what?

It was the same everywhere. People bought all kinds of things, things they didn't want or need.

'This is stupid,' everyone said. Then they bought something too. No one knew how to stop. Shopping was the only thing people talked about – in the street, on the news.

People started to feel afraid. Everybody spent too much money. Doctors, scientists, politicians all talked about it. Some people thought it was a new virus.

And was it? Nobody knew. But people shopped online all the time now. They didn't have the money to pay for their shopping. But that didn't stop them. People spent money they didn't have, and they just bought too much. Soon, their houses were too small for the hundreds of things that they bought. Many of these things never came out of their boxes.

*   *   *

'What is going on?' Louise asked herself. 'Now I'm home from my holiday, and everything is different. Something is wrong. But what?'

Louise went to the computer to read her emails. When she was on holiday, she didn't use the computer. But she knew that her parents read their emails every day. Was there some important news that she didn't know about?

Inez saw Louise sit down at the computer.

'Can I look?' asked Inez. 'I'm waiting for an email.'

'OK, Mum,' said Louise. She got up, but she stayed next to her mother. Inez opened her emails. Louise watched her mother's face. Her mother's eyes were very big as she read one of her emails.

Then Inez jumped up. 'OK,' she said. 'You can look at your email now, Louise.'

'Why was Mum different when she read that email?' thought Louise. She looked at the address of her mother's email. It was from an internet shopping company. But Louise didn't open it, because then Inez came back. She had her credit card in her hand. 'Is she going to buy more things?' thought Louise.

'I must buy that nice purple shirt for Joe,' said Inez, and she sat down in front of the computer again.

Purple? Louise knew her Dad hated purple. This was all wrong! What was in that email?

'Er... I think there's something wrong with the computer,' said Louise. 'Let me look at it, Mum.'

'OK,' said Inez. 'I can come back later.'

Louise started work.

*　　*　　*

'Mum, Dad! There's an email for you! It says it's very important!' Louise ran into the kitchen, with the computer in her hands.

Joe and Inez opened the email and looked at it. Their eyes closed and they didn't speak or move. Then, after a few minutes, they opened their eyes and looked at Louise.

'What? Where are we? What did those emails *do* to us?' asked Joe.

'It's OK now, Dad,' said Louise. 'That internet shopping company put things in the emails. They put ideas in your head that you didn't know about. It was like a computer virus, but it worked on people. So everyone bought all those things they didn't need. Not very nice. All I did was change the message. Easy, really.'

'Did you really do it, Louise?' asked Inez.

'Of course I did. No internet company can stop me. This afternoon I changed the email program. This email's going to take the virus away when people open it. The internet company can't do anything about it,' said Louise.

Joe and Inez looked around at all the things that were still in their boxes. There were salad bowls and things for the garden, shoes and clothes, books and music – lots of things they didn't need. They laughed.

'The internet company thought it knew everything,' said Louise. 'But it didn't!'

'Louise, do you like chocolate cakes?' said Inez with a smile.

'Of course! Why, Mum?' asked Louise.

'Because I bought forty of them and they're in the kitchen!' said Inez.

And they all laughed.

A Flower for Lumus

Place: Paris
Year: 2106

'Sometimes I forget who the helpers really are,' said Fleur to
Lumus Chevalier. 'They're very like us. I don't know. Is being
like us a good thing? I just don't know.'

'Don't think about the helpers, Fleur,' Lumus answered.
'Not when it makes you feel bad.'

'How can I feel bad?' said Fleur with a little smile. 'You're
always there for me.' She put down her coffee and kissed
him.

Lumus smiled. 'And you for me, Fleur.'

A waiter came to their table. 'More coffee?' he asked them. The waiter was one of many waiters at the hotel. He wasn't tall or short, and he had dark hair. All the waiters were just like him. They all looked the same.

Fleur asked for more coffee but Lumus didn't. The waiter walked away. Fleur and Lumus watched him. Fleur drank some coffee, then she put her cup down.

'Why don't they have fat waiters?' she asked. 'Or thin waiters? Why do they all look the same?'

'We read about it, Fleur,' said Lumus. 'Do you remember? We read about it before we came here. It was in the little book about the hotel. They all look the same because they're waiters. Nobody wants waiters who look different. People want to eat their meal and talk. They don't want to look at lots of different waiters.'

'You know what, Lumus?' said Fleur. 'I don't like looking at them at all. They look like real people. They speak like real people. I don't know. Some of them think they are real people. They eat and drink like you and me. But it's not the same. They're not real people at all. I don't like that.'

Lumus said nothing. Fleur said lots of things about the helpers. Everybody knew that helpers looked like people. But they weren't people. Was it right for Fleur to think of them like that? He didn't like her to feel bad. He wanted her to be happy. Just like the old days. He must do something about that. But what?

'Why don't we go for a walk?' he asked. 'The Sun Room's open now. We can see flowers and trees. Animals too. You always like that!'

'You're right,' said Fleur. 'I do. Let's go.'

*　　*　　*

People had nowhere to walk outside now. It was too expensive. Everybody lived in buildings of some kind – they didn't go outside. There wasn't room for people like Fleur and Lumus to walk outside. Not any more.

But Fleur didn't see why anyone went outside. Not now. There wasn't a lot to see. Where were the animals? Gone. Where were the trees? Gone. Trees and animals were only in the Sun Rooms now. But they weren't like the old trees and animals. Not really. And tickets for the Sun Rooms weren't cheap.

Sun Rooms were big rooms where you went for a walk. Computers made everything. Trees, animals, birds – everything. You made your own world in a Sun Room. You made the world you wanted. You bought a ticket at the door and asked for the things you wanted to see. Big flowers, little flowers, trees with green leaves, trees with red leaves, animals – it was up to you. The computers did it all for you.

The Sun Room was beautiful. Fleur and Lumus went in. They walked hand in hand on the grass. They always chose grass and flowers. They liked the feel of grass under their feet. The Room felt good – not too cold, not too hot. A deer walked next to them. Lumus put his hand on its head. There were flowers in many different colours in the grass.

Lumus took some flowers. 'Smell these,' he said. 'Aren't they beautiful?'

'Yes, they are,' Fleur answered. 'Come on, I want to take some of these flowers with us.'

'We can't, Fleur,' said Lumus. 'We can't take things out of the Sun Room. Anyway, they aren't real flowers.'

'Oh, yes,' said Fleur sadly. 'I forgot.'

'Let's go back now.' Lumus knew when Fleur was sad. He took her hand and they went back to their room.

There was a photograph on a small table next to the bed. It was Fleur and Lumus on the day they were married. They were both young. Fleur had long yellow hair. She looked very happy. Her dress was pink. She was twenty-three years old. Lumus was twenty-nine. There was a big smile on his face too. He was good-looking: tall, with dark hair and brown eyes.

But that was in 2086. Now it was 2106. Fleur was still in love with the Lumus in the picture.

'You look tired, Lumus,' she said. 'Why don't you sleep for half an hour?'

'Yes, I am tired,' Lumus answered. 'But are you OK? Don't you want a cup of tea?'

'I'm OK,' smiled Fleur. 'You go and have a sleep.'

Lumus went to sleep right away. Fleur looked at him. He was good-looking with dark hair. He was wearing a suit just like the one in the photograph. He didn't look a day over twenty-nine. She looked at her face and pink dress in the mirror. She looked very good for a woman of forty-three. But she didn't look young, like him. She looked at Lumus again and put her hand on his. It was warm. Then she used the phone.

'Hello, is that The Helper Company? Yes, it's about my helper. Yes, Lumus Chevalier, born 2057, died 2089. Yes, this is about Lumus number four.'

Fleur looked at the photograph by the bed as she spoke. Her eyes were wet.

'This helper was nice. He was the nicest of all of them. But it's still not the same. It can't be the same ...'

Fleur put the telephone down and looked at Lumus. She kissed him and put a paper flower on the bed, next to his head. Then she put her hand on the back of his neck.

And she turned him off.

Zima's Last Dream

Place: our world
Time: fifteen hundred years from now

Water everywhere. That's all Zima can see from the window. She's high up in a tall building, and all she can see is water. But you can't drink it. There are too many bad things in it. Nobody drinks it. Zima doesn't like to think about the water, but there are some things she *can't* forget.

Zima remembers one thing. Many years ago, there was good, clean water for people to drink. Water that wasn't dirty. But clean water was expensive then. You bought it in bottles.

People with a lot of money weren't thirsty. But when you had no money, you just tried to get the bad things out of the dirty water. And that wasn't easy.

But Zima also remembers happy times. When she was a girl, her family was rich. She drank good water all the time, and she ate good food too. She was never hungry or thirsty. But that was many years ago.

'I remember!' Zima thinks. 'Animals, trees, cities! Lots of people. And my husband! My children!'

Zima feels happy. She tries to remember her family. But she's tired. Remembering things always makes her tired. It was all many years ago. She forgets a lot now. And the animals, and the trees? They're all gone. All of them.

'All those beautiful things are gone,' Zima thinks. 'But I want to remember them!'

Zima tries, but it's no good. She can't remember.

Zima thinks of all the people in the world. Where are they? Gone. She remembers and she feels afraid.

Then she remembers a man called Niko. She liked Niko. He was important in her life. But he's gone now. When did he go? Was it years ago? She doesn't know. She forgets what he looked like.

Zima can't remember *her* face. She doesn't know what she looks like. She feels sad. All the pictures in her head – the pictures of her life – are going away. It isn't easy to think of them now. It makes her tired. She tries to see the pictures again. But she can't. The pictures leave her head all the time now.

Zima doesn't eat or drink now. She can't. What is it like to be thirsty? Or hungry? It isn't easy for her to remember. She knows she liked good food and good water. But why?

Zima looks out of the window. She looks out every day. She always sees just dark blue water. And sometimes the sun. That's all there is. There are still some pictures in her head. She tries to keep them. But they all go away from her. She wants to catch the pictures in her fingers. But she can't.

Zima thinks. She remembers something. Her fingers. She had fingers… but does she have them now? She looks but she can't see them. When did she last see her fingers? She can't remember.

*   *   *

A thousand years ago the Machines came. The Machines walked and talked. The Machines thought and had ideas. They didn't like what the Old Ones did.

The world was old, dirty and tired. It was dying because of the Old Ones, because they didn't think about their world. The Machines knew what to do. They wanted to stop the Old Ones and change their world.

The Machines took over the world. They didn't want a dead world, and they didn't need the Old Ones.

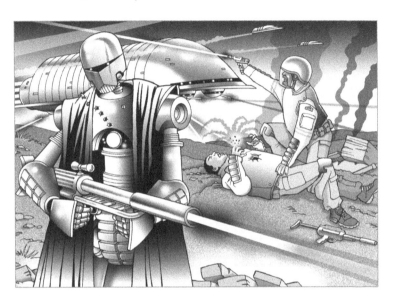

There was only one thing they wanted from the Old Ones. The Machines wanted to know what the Old Ones knew. They needed ideas. Computers didn't tell them everything. The brains of the Old Ones had many ideas inside them. The Machines wanted their ideas.

The Machines kept millions of brains. The brains were all in glass bottles, but they weren't dead. There were thousands – no, millions of pictures and dreams in the brains. The Machines took all the pictures and dreams of the Old Ones.

Now it was a world of machines, and there weren't many living things – no fish or animals. But the Machines wanted to know about Life. Where did it come from? The Machines thought that the Old Ones were interesting. Did they make the first Machines? The answer was in the brains.

'Who made us?' The Machines wanted an answer. They took everything from the brains of the Old Ones. They took all the words and pictures. They took more and more, and soon the brains had no more ideas in them. Then the brains died, and the Old Ones died too. But still the Machines had no answer to their question.

Last week, there were only two Old Ones left in the world. There was the brain of a man called Niko, and the brain of a woman called Zima. The two brains were very old, and there wasn't very much life in them.

Niko and Zima thought they were living people again. They saw the water in front of them. The eye in their brains also saw pictures from their past. Computers took every picture from their brains. Niko and Zima didn't know this. They just looked at the water and dreamed.

Then Niko's brain died. Niko was dead. Zima didn't know this. She didn't see Niko, dead, in the bottle next to her. She felt very sad, but she didn't know why.

*   *   *

That was last week. Now Zima's remembering her past. She remembers animals. She saw them on TV when she was a girl. Some were big, like the animal that was black and orange with big teeth. Some were small and moved quickly on the grass or in the air. Fish moved in the water. They were beautiful.

But she never saw these animals in real life, she only saw them on TV. Near her house, she saw cows and sheep. She liked them. But she didn't like some of the little living things she often saw. What were they called? Zima thinks. Then she remembers… insects! They came from dark places and weren't beautiful at all. She was afraid of them.

But she doesn't see anything much now. She tries to bring pictures into her head. She knows that pictures are all she has. Pictures and words. But she can't always remember them.

Now Zima's the last Old One. The Machines must take everything they can. They want an answer to their question. Can Zima's brain give them the answer?

The Machines do everything they can to make Zima think. They want the pictures in her brain. They want her to dream. It is, they know, the last dream she's going to have. She's the last of the Old Ones, and everything in her brain – her dreams and her ideas, every little thing that she remembers – is very important for the Machines. They try again, for the last time. Think, Zima, think! The Machines watch and wait.

*   *   *

Zima has a dream. She knows it's a dream. Everything's a dream, isn't it? But this dream is beautiful. She sees her family. She sees Niko, the husband she loves. She sees her children and feels nothing but love. She was happy when she was with them.

She sees cities with thousands of people in them. People laugh and dance. People live and die. She remembers now. When she was an Old One, she lived in a beautiful world. Where is it now? Can she make the world beautiful again? What can she do? Where is she now?

Then she feels something. It feels like a hand on her brain… and she forgets everything. She looks out at the water. She thinks she sees birds fly and call out to her. She thinks she sees fish come out of the water and go back again. The water's dark blue. Is it real?

Then she sees Niko. He's tall, and he's smiling at her. He calls her name. And Zima remembers love. Her world is beautiful again.

Zima's tired but she's happy. Her one eye closes. She sleeps.

Cambridge English Readers

Look out for other titles in this series:

Level 1

Help!
by Philip Prowse

Frank Wormold is a writer. To help him finish one of his stories, he starts to use a computer. But the computer gives him more help than he wants.

Parallel
by Colin Campbell

'Max sat on his bed. There was a gun beside him. The gun was still warm.'
Max kills people for money. But one day he goes to a new world and his life changes.

Blood Diamonds
by Richard MacAndrew

Van Delft is a businessman. He buys and sells things in many countries. But some people think he also buys and sells guns … and diamonds.
Kirkpatrick and Shepherd are two journalists. They are writing a front-page story – about blood diamonds. Is Van Delft the man they want?

John Doe
by Antoinette Moses

The man they call John Doe lies in a hospital bed. He watches and thinks but says nothing. The doctor wants to know who he is. But John Doe doesn't answer his questions. Then, after John Doe leaves the hospital, the doctor finds out more about him than just his real name.

Inspector Logan
by Richard MacAndrew

'When did your wife go out?' asked Jenny Logan.

She looked at the man across the table from her.

'Yesterday,' he replied.

'And she didn't come home last night?'

'That's right,' said the man.

It was Jenny Logan's first day as a police inspector. This was her first murder.

Next Door to Love
by Margaret Johnson

'You need to go out, Stella,' my best friend often told me. 'You need to meet new people. New men.'

But I didn't want to meet new men, and I didn't want a boyfriend.

Then Tony came to live in the house next door and everything changed.

Bad Love
by Sue Leather

'Dr. Jack Daly?' Judy said. 'He's famous.'

'I don't often like famous people,' I said.

'Oh, come on, Detective Laine!'

One week later Daly is dead and Flick Laine is looking for his killer.

The Big Picture
by Sue Leather

Ken Harada takes photos for newspapers. But life gets dangerous when Ken takes a photo of a sumo star. Someone wants the photo badly. But who? And why?

Level 2

Circle Games
by Frank Brennan

Five stories to make you smile – and think: a Chinese lion dancer turns round and round; an old wooden wheel sits on an English pub wall; an American teenager makes a new wheel for a car; a bicycle taxi driver in Singapore helps a sick girl; and an English student finds a strange, and very old, disc.

Different Worlds
by Margaret Johnson

'In my world there are no birds singing. There are no noisy men working on the roads. No babies crying.'

Sam is like any other teenage girl except that she was born deaf. Now she is in love with Jim, but are their worlds too different?

Within High Fences
by Penny Hancock

'There was nothing different about that night. But that night, my life started to change. It's the night when Nancy meets George. But it isn't easy for them to be together. There's Nancy's job and her boyfriend. And will George have to return to his own country?

Jojo's Story
by Antoinette Moses

'There aren't any more days. There's just time. Time when it's dark and time when it's light. Everything is dead, so why not days too?'

Everyone in Jojo's village is dead, and ten-year-old Jojo is alone.